T0246601

"A wonderful, rewarding book."
  — *The Philadelphia Inquirer*

"This book is superb. . . . Simple in its language, spare in its style, *Braided Creek* presents dozens of short poems that resonate with truth, pain and radiance."
  — *The Kansas City Star*

"Seamless, poignant and profound."
  — *The Wichita Eagle*

"These little gems prove that less is often more."
  — *Library Journal*

"There are poems on the natural world . . . aging, dying, friendship, love and eros. There is abundant humor. . . . There also is distilled wisdom."
  — *Houston Chronicle*

"So what we have here is a small book of finely etched verse by two experienced poets. It is something that many readers will want to carry around with them . . . *Braided Creek* is a vademecum or field guide for the soul."
  — *The Bloomsbury Review*

"Harrison and Kooser's conversation braids courage, contemplation and a clear look at the trials and rewards of life."
—*Sunday News* (Lancaster)

"*Braided Creek* is a unique and wonderful book composed of unattributed, haiku-like, often hilarious, poems which the longtime friends exchanged through the mail while Kooser was undergoing treatment for cancer."
—Indiana Public Media

"Here's a book of glorious, intimate tidbits. . . . Filled with such small yet expansive moments, perfectly defined."
—*The Memphis Commercial Appeal*

Braided Creek

BRAIDED CREEK

A Conversation in Poetry

EXPANDED ANNIVERSARY EDITION

Ted Kooser and Jim Harrison

Foreword by Naomi Shihab Nye
Afterword by Ted Kooser

Copper Canyon Press
Port Townsend, Washington

Grateful acknowledgment to the estate of Russell Chatham for the generous permission to use a detail from the painting *Spring Creek* on the front cover.

Special thanks to Keil Dumsch for permission to use his photograph of Jim and Linda Harrison's mailbox on the back cover.

Bows of gratitude to Don J. Usner for permission to use his photograph of Ted and Jim enjoying each other's company at a Lannan Foundation reading in Santa Fe.

Several poems from *Braided Creek* first appeared in the chapbook *A Conversation*, published in 2002 by Aralia Press.

Copper Canyon Press is in residence at Fort Worden State Park in Port Townsend, Washington, under the auspices of Centrum. Centrum is a gathering place for artists and creative thinkers from around the world, students of all ages and backgrounds, and audiences seeking extraordinary cultural enrichment.

LIBRARY OF CONGRESS CATALOGING-IN-PUBLICATION DATA
Names: Kooser, Ted, author. | Harrison, Jim, 1937–2016, author. | Nye, Naomi Shihab, writer of foreword.
Title: Braided creek : a conversation in poetry / Ted Kooser and Jim Harrison ; foreword by Naomi Shihab Nye ; afterword by Ted Kooser.
Description: Expanded anniversary edition. | Port Townsend, Washington : Copper Canyon Press, 2023. |
Summary: "An expanded anniversary edition of a collection of poems by Ted Kooser and Jim Harrison"— Provided by publisher.
Identifiers: LCCN 2022046797 (print) | LCN 2022046798 (ebook) | ISBN 9781556596797 (hardcover) | ISBN 9781619320918 (epub)
Subjects: LCGFT: Poetry.
Classification: LCC PS3561.O6 B73 2023 (print) | LCC PS3561.06 (ebook) | DDC 811/.54—dc23/eng/20230118
LC record available at https://lccn.loc.gov/2022046797
LC ebook record available at https://lccn.loc.gov/2022046798

9 8 7 6 5 4 3 2 FIRST PRINTING

COPPER CANYON PRESS
Post Office Box 271
Port Townsend, Washington 98368
www.coppercanyonpress.org

MIX
Paper from
responsible sources
FSC® C011935

to Dan Gerber

Everybody allows that the talent of writing agreeable letters is peculiarly female.

JANE AUSTEN, *Northanger Abbey*

Little Rocket Ship of Wonders

Braided Creek: A Conversation in Poetry is one of the dearest, most appealing books ever published. These poems are tiny, delicious American haiku-like poems affectionately exchanged between two friends, Ted Kooser and Jim Harrison, great writers, during a time of support. Ted was recovering from a serious illness, Jim kept sending small poems to his rural mailbox, and Ted replied in kind. This generous and nourishing correspondence went on privately for years, and then the poets decided to share their poems with the reading public. *Thank goodness!*

Each page of *Braided Creek* offers instant transporting power for a reader's mind. One might ask, how does a tiny poem refresh consciousness so well? Is it the wide space around the lines? The simple riveting focus required? The essential understatement? This slim volume acts as a palate cleanser, a spirit booster, a little rocket ship of wonders. I adore the sense of comfortable congeniality, the tender eye toward the smallest details, the boots and ants and worms and stars, the wistfulness, the mice and myriad memories woven through. It's a funny book, full of joy and wisdom and enduring fascination.

Reading this book for the first time nearly twenty years ago, I fell so in love with it, I ordered twenty more copies from Copper Canyon Press, to give to friends—ranchers, architects, classroom teachers—and people loved it. I bought ten more copies. Then twenty more. I'd never purchased so many copies of a single book. Some recipients said they needed another copy immediately, to give to someone else, and I would happily provide one. One friend said he'd been feeling bleak about human communication and this slender little book restored his love for words. Some said they had begun similar correspondence chains with writing friends. Teachers agreed that sharing a few of these poems before student writing sessions magically stimulated them. Contagious clarity embodied! Over the years, reading *Braided Creek* poems aloud in writing workshops, I keep finding startling images and leaps I've never noticed before. Has the book changed? Have I? These poems that I know so well keep waking me up. And every time, I love that the two friends did not claim authorship over the individual poems by placing their names on them. Ted told me once that some reviewers speculated over who wrote which poem, and got it wrong every time.

Twenty years since *Braided Creek* was first printed, it resonates even more deeply.

> So much to live for.
> Each rope rings
> a different bell.

We've survived longer, experienced more grief and change, lost faith in our country and perhaps regained it, worried deeply, been horrified by gun violence and baffled by liars in power, made new friends, possibly experienced illness ourselves, and had to remind ourselves of the preciousness of every day and individual memory more than once. What a celebration that *Braided Creek* returns to us now in a fresh anniversary edition; we need these poems just as much as we ever did, if not more. Your attention span has shrunk? You need wisdom more desperately? Here's the book for you. May you too be ignited by the finely tuned, electrically charged poetic minds of Ted Kooser and the late Jim Harrison, and may you find herein your own horizons of pleasure.

Naomi Shihab Nye, Young People's
Poet Laureate, Poetry Foundation
Summer 2022

BRAIDED CREEK

How one old tire leans up against
another, the breath gone out of both.

Old friend,
perhaps we work too hard
at being remembered.

Which way will the creek
run when time ends?
Don't ask me until
this wine bottle is empty.

While my bowl is still half full,
you can eat out of it too,
and when it is empty,
just bury it out in the flowers.

3

All those years
I had in my pocket.
I spent them,
nickel-and-dime.

Each clock tick falls
like a raindrop,
right through the floor
as if it were nothing.

In the morning light,
the doorknob, cold with dew.

The Pilot Razor Point pen is my
compass, watch, and soul chaser.
Thousands of miles of black squiggles.

Under the storyteller's hat
are many heads, all troubled.

At dawn, a rabbit stretches tall
to eat the red asparagus berries.

The big fat garter snake
emerged from the gas-stove burner
where she had coiled around the pilot light
for warmth on a cold night.

Straining on the toilet
we learn how
the lightning bug feels.

For sixty-three years I've ground myself
within this karmic mortar. Yesterday I washed
it out and put it high on the pantry shelf.

All I want to be
is a thousand blackbirds
bursting from a tree,
seeding the sky.

Republicans think that all over the world
darker-skinned people are having more fun
than they are. It's largely true.

Faucet dripping into a pan,
dog lapping water,
the same sweet music.

The nuthatch is in business
on the tree trunk,
fortunes up and down.

Oh what dew
these mortals be.
Dawn to dark.
One long breath.

The wit of the corpse
is lost on the lid of the coffin.

A book on the arm of my chair
and the morning before me.

Everyone thought I'd die
in my twenties, thirties, forties, fifties.
This can't go on forever.

The graduates wear mortarboards
but haven't learned to use a trowel.

There are mornings
when everything brims with promise,
even my empty cup.

Two squirrels fight
to near death,
red blood flecking green grass,
while chipmunks continue feeding.

What pleasure: a new straw hat
with a green brim to look through!

Rowing across the lake
all the dragonflies are screwing.
Stop it. It's Sunday.

Throw out the anchor
unattached to a rope.
Heart lifts as it sinks.
Out of my mind at last.

On every topographic map,
the fingerprints of God.

When we were very poor one spring
I fished a snowy river and caught
a big trout. It changed our lives
that day: eating, drinking, singing, dancing.

Lost: Ambition.
Found: A good book,
an old sweater,
loose shoes.

Years ago
when I became tough as a nail
I became a nail.

An old song from my youth:
"I'm going to live, live, live
until I die." Well, perhaps not.

Still at times I'm a dumb little boy
fishing from a rowboat in the rain
wanting to give the family a fish dinner.

Only today
I heard
the river
within the river.

Clear summer dawn,
first sun steams moisture
redly off the cabin roof,
a cold fire. Passing raven
eyeballs it with a *quawk*.

The rabbit is born
prepared for listening,
the poet just for talk.

As a boy when desperate I'd pray with bare knees
on the cold floor. I still do,
but from the window I look like an old man.

Two buzzards
perched on a hay bale
and a third just gliding in.

I want to describe my life in hushed tones
like a TV nature program. *Dawn in the north.*
His nose stalks the air for newborn coffee.

Turtle has just one plan
at a time, and every cell
buys into it.

The biomass of ants,
their total weight on Earth,
exceeds our own.
They welcome us to their world
of small homes, hard work, big women.

But the seventeen-year cicada
has only one syllable.

What prizes and awards will I get for revealing
the location of the human soul? As Nixon said,
I know how to win the war but I'm not telling.

Some days
one needs to hide
from possibility.

She climbed the green-leafed apple tree
in her green Sunday dress. Her white panties
were white as the moon above brown legs.

Is this poem a pebble,
or a raindrop coated with dust?

Each time I go outside the world
is different. This has happened
all my life.

When I found my tracks in the snow
I followed, thinking that they might
lead me back to where I was. But
they turned the wrong way and went on.

I schlump around the farm
in dirty, insulated coveralls
checking the private lives of mice.

I heard the lake cheeping
under the ice, too weak
to break through the shell.

Nothing to do.
Nowhere to go.
The moth just drowned
in the whiskey glass.
This is heaven.

The old dog tries
a dozen ways of lying down,
then settles on the last.

Wind in the chimney
turns on its heel
without crushing the ashes.

Way out in the local wilderness
the only human tracks are mine, left foot
pigeon-toed, aimless.

Trust snow to keep a secret.

Old white soup bowl
chipped like a tooth,
one of us is always empty.

I used to have time by the ass
but now I share it in common
and it's going away.

These legs
are wearing out.
Uphill, downhill.
They'll love
their flat earth rest.

Old centipede
can't keep himself
from leaving.

My dog girlfriend Rose was lost
for three endless days and nights
during which I uncontrollably sobbed.

Fear is a swallow
in a boarded-up warehouse,
seeking a window out.

The brown stumps
of my old teeth
don't send up shoots
in spring.

In New York
on a wet
and bitter street
I heard a crow from home.

Mouse nest in the toe of my boot,
have I been gone that long?

I haven't forgotten
to look in the mirror,
I just don't
do it anymore.

When Time picks apples,
it eats them with the yellow teeth
of bees.

We flap our gums, our wattles, our
featherless wings in non-native air
to avoid being planted in earth,
watching the bellies of passing birds.

On its stand on the empty stage
the tuba with its big brass ear
enjoys the silence.

So what if women
no longer smile to see me?
I smile to see them!

Why do I behave so badly?
Just because. That's still
a good answer.

Now an outlander, once a poet in NY
crisscrossing Gotham for food and drink,
the souls of Lorca and Crane a daily solstice.

Open the shoe-store door
and a bell rings:
two shoehorns on a shoelace.

Let go of the mind, the thousand blue
story fragments we tell ourselves
each day to keep the world underfoot.

How foolish the houseplant looks
as it offers its droopy leaves
like hands to be kissed.

I trace my noble ancestry back
to the first seed, the first cell
that emerged reluctantly from the void.

The crow comes from
a broken home.
She is so loud because
no one will listen.

Dog days
for me and the dogs,
afloat clockwise
in the river's eddy.

The deer hung flapping
high on the buffalo fence,
pushed by an inner wind.

The pigeon
has swallowed a fountain!
Listen!

The goofy young bald eagle
is ignored by the seagulls and ravens
as these enemies share
a barrel of fish heads and guts.

On Everest there are pink concealed
gnats that when falling
learn decisively that they can't fly.

Surely someone will help
the mourning mourning dove,
but who, but who?

Trees stay in place.
Fish spend a lifetime underwater.
Our last track is a skull.

A coffin handle
leaves a lasting impression
on a hand.

Oh the dark, rank, brackish rut
of money. The news from the inside
is fine. Outside, a sucking cold vacuum.

A nephew rubs the sore feet
of his aunt,
and the rope that lifts us all toward grace
creaks in the pulley.

The cups of the tulips
tip forward, spilling their snow.

Sometimes my big front teeth bite
my lower lip and my food gets bloody.
What is this argument all about?

"Do you feel your age?" she asked,
so I squeezed my age till it hurt,
then set it free.

Rising from a cramped position
before the fireplace I discover
that there's blood in my legs.

So much to live for.
Each rope rings
a different bell.

Fifty-two degrees at noon, July 2.
At the senior citizens' carwash
all the oldsters try to look vigorous.

The mirror, backed in black,
and grief behind each face.

When you drink from dawn's light
you see the bottom of the cup.

The weeping man
pulls off his glasses, holds them out
to keep them dry.

I am wherever I find myself to be,
of all places. At 6 a.m. the Paris lights
shine through the cool November rain.
Only a few hours ago there was a moon.

My new trifocals hurt my nose.
All that lifting them up and down
just to find my way.

The fat snake's gone this year.
She's been transplanted to a place
she won't hear my startled yelp
when she emerges from the stove top.

Winter knows
when a man's pockets
are empty.

Old willow
taps the river
with his cane.

I was paralyzed from the waist up
for three months. My feet walked me.
The birds all turned brown. I fell
out of a tree I hadn't climbed.

An empty boat
will volunteer for anything.

When the dollhouse was built in a month's work
a red ghost was trapped in a tiny closet.
You can hear its breathing a thousand miles.

Gentle readers, tomorrow I undergo
radical brain surgery, but don't worry.
Win some. Lose some. Mostly ties.

Wanted: Looking for owl roosts
for pellets for Science project.
Call Marli.

In each of my cells Dad and Mom
are still doing their jobs. As always,
Dad says *yes*, Mom *no*. I split the difference
and feel deep sympathy for my children.

At the tip of memory's
great funnel cloud
is the nib of a pen.

At my cabin
to write a poem
is to throw an egg across
the narrow river into the trees.

A dozen dead houseflies,
bits of green glass from the bottle
of summer, smashed on the sill.

Getting older I'm much better at watching
rain. I skip counting individual drops
in favor of the general feeling of rain.

Like a fist, the toad
knocks on the dirt road
wanting in.

Strange world indeed:
a poet keeping himself awake
to write about insomnia.

The sparrow is not busy,
but hungry.

I remember being a cellular oyster
in a tiny geode before being prodded
into a world of lilacs and blood.

Next to a gravestone,
a green tin cup
brimful of shadows.
Must we drink?

There is just one of us.
Already you are what you are.
Old rooster crowing with a stretched neck.

I might have been a welder,
kneeling at a fountain of sparks
in my mask of stars.

The moon put her white hands
on my shoulders, looked into my face,
and without a word
sent me on into the night.

Coming home late from the tavern.
A mouse has drowned in the toilet.
A metaphor of the poet, I think.
But no, the death of a glorious mouse.

The drunken man
spills most of his importance
on his shoes.

After carefully listing my 10,000 illusions
I noticed that nearly all that I found
in the depths was lost in the shallows.

Raindrops on your glasses;
there you go again,
reading the clouds.

Dewdrops are the dreams
of the grass. They linger, shining,
into the morning.

If you can awaken
inside the familiar
and discover it strange
you need never leave home.

The birds,
confused by rain clouds,
think it's evening.

Another spring,
and a long trail of grease ants
over the breadboard.

The girl with blue shorts and brown legs
the color of the dog beside her
ran through the green orchard
kicking her butt with her own heels.

Lost for a while,
I found her name
when I scratched through
my hair.

To prevent leakage,
immerse yourself in clouds and birds,
a jubilant drift downward.

With her brush, the artist
touches one part of her life
with another.

You told me you couldn't see
a better day coming,
so I gave you my eyes.

How can Lorca say he's only the pulse
of a wound that probes to the opposite side?
I'm wondering if he ever rowed a boat backwards.

The black sleeve falls back
from the scalded fist:
a turkey vulture.

At 62 I've outlived 95 percent
of the world. I'll be home
just before dark.

All my life
I've been in the caboose
with blind glands
running the locomotive.

Letters from beautiful women.
What do they tell me?

Woodpecker,
why so much effort
for such little gain?

In Mexico the big, lovely
woman took off her blue outfit
becoming a normal woman
only more so.

The way a springer spaniel
hops through deep grass,
I was once a lover like that.

When she left me
I stood out in the thunderstorm,
hoping to be destroyed by lightning.
It missed, first left, then right.

When a hammer sings
its head is loose.

Actresses I've known grow younger
while I don't, but after my Vietnam head
wounds, I won three Olympic gold medals.

The one-eyed man must be fearful
of being taken for a birdhouse.

As a child I loved to square-dance,
a junior beast sniffing my fingers
after they touched a new girl's hand.

Reading poetry late at night
to try to come back to life.
Almost but not quite.

Now it's the body's dog, pain,
barking and barking.
A stranger has come to the gate
with an empty sack.

The hay in the loft
misses the night sky,
so the old roof
leaks a few stars.

Rain clouds gone,
and muddy paw prints
on the moon.

I've never learned from experience.
What else is there? you ask.
How about ninety billion galaxies.

Even a very dark, starless night
can grow a little darker. A bat
has just switched off a firefly.

What is it the wind has lost
that she keeps looking for
under each leaf?

I grow older.
I still like women, but mostly
I like Mexican food.

Sleeping on my right side I think
of God. On my left side, sex.
On my back I snore with my dog.

Some nights are three nights long,
some days a mere noon hour, then whistled
back to work, the heart dredging sludge.

The nightmare we waken from,
grateful, is somebody else's life.

Mirrors have always given the wrong
impression of me. So do other people.
So do I. Let's stop this right now.

The face you look out of
is never the face
your lover looks into.

The crumpled candy wrapper
is just another flower
to the rain.

How can I disappoint myself?
How many are within this brown
and wrinkled skin? Just one in pieces.

The stones turn their backs to us.
Our lives are light as flyspecks.

What has become
of the great hunter?
Today he won't kill flies.

Out in a field, an immense empty
pasture, clouds of leaves fell
from no visible trees. I was scared.

God's hand is cupped
over the crickety heart
of the turtle.

At the cabin I left the canola bottle open
and eleven mice drowned in this oil bath.
I had invented the mouse atom bomb.

The firefly's one word:
darkness!

A bumblebee,
a straggly rosebush
staining the air with her scent.
A blue and black butterfly—
too many *B*s but life is like that.

How tall would I be
without my enemies
to measure me?

One grows tired of the hoax of up
and down. Jesus descended into a universe
of neither perfect lines, squares, nor circles.

You step in the same river once only
for an instant. Panhandle time with
the bruised fingers of what might have been.

"Charred beyond recognition" is bad news.
Yet it happens to us all. Ashes
have never returned to wood.

In an egg yolk,
an artery fine as the touch
of a feather.

The cow dogs caught their first jackrabbit.
Ace, the big male, is curled in the dirt
growling to protect his trophy, the bloody ears.

How lucky in one life to see
the sun lift a cloud from a pool!

This slender blue thread,
if anything,
connects everything.

The old man's eyes are huge
behind new glasses. Look!
Young women everywhere!

The Great Gourmand rows his boat
all day on a peanut butter sandwich
and warm water.

At my age,
even in airports,
why would you wish
time to move faster?

The clock stopped at 5:30 for three months.
Now it's always time to quit work,
have a drink, cook dinner.

The butterfly
jots a note on the wind
to remind itself of something.

How can it be
that everyone my age
is older than I?

Twisted my ankle
until it's blue.
Now I can feel my heart
beating in my foot.

How attentive the big bear resting his chin
on the bird feeder, an eye rolling toward my window
to see if he has permission for sunflower seeds.

On my desk two
indisputably great creations:
duct tape and saltine crackers.

In a pasture, wild turkeys
flip cow pies, looking for bugs.

Suddenly my clocks agree.
One has been stopped for several
months, but twice a day
they have this tender moment.

In deer season,
walking in the woods,
I sing like Pavarotti.

"What I would do for wisdom,"
I cried out as a young man.
Evidently not much. Or so it seems.
Even on walks I follow the dog.

The owl is a bronze urn of ashes
till one of the round seals blinks.

Crow with a red beak
looks over his shoulder.

After rowing my blue and brown boat
for three hours I liked the world again,
the two loons close by, the theory of red wine.

Waited all day for the moon to rise.
It just happened.
I can't believe my luck.

I saw a black butterfly
as big as a raven
flapping through the night.
Maybe it was an owl.

Ten mousetraps in the cellar
and one dead mouse.
Pretty good odds for living.

In 1947 a single gold nugget was found
hereabouts. Old men still look for a second one.
In between life has passed.

In my garden
the late sun glows
through a rabbit's ears.

Midday silence is different
from nighttime silence.
I can't tell you how.

Between the four pads
of a dog's foot,
the fragrance of grass.

July, and fat black flies
so slow you can bat them
right out of the air.

Dead raccoon, legs in the air,
washes his paws in the sky.

Flecks of foam
on the fountain's lips
as it reads aloud from
the scripture of water.

This morning,
fish bleed into nacreous clouds
and an iron bird walks to town
on the bottom of the river.

I'm so pleased that Yeats
never got off his stilts
though I have only one.

I have used up more than
20,000 days waiting to see
what the next would bring.

It's hard to believe there's a skeleton
inside us, not certainly in the beautiful
girl getting out of her red car.

Elaborate is the courtliness
of the imagination, on one sore knee
before beauty.

When I touched her long feet
I stopped walking.
When I tasted her mouth
I quit eating.

When I watched her hands
as she peeled a potato,
I gave up everything I owned.

I have grown old, and know
how an owl feels,
seeing a man with a lantern.

November cold. Hey, grasshopper!
What goes? Once all that armor
weighed nothing!

In winter, don't ever
touch your tongue
to someone cold.

Fresh snow standing deep
on the phone wire. If you call me,
speak softly.

Well before dawn I woke
up crying because my teeth hurt.
Lucky for me there was soothing rain
on the cabin roof.

I woke up as nothing. Now start piling
it on. No. Yes. No. Maybe. Indoors.
Outdoors. Me. You. Her corpse said stop.

Birds and bugs
flying left and right.
Always the question,
What to do next?

The wasp
has built his palace
in a bell.

Life has always yelled at me,
"Get your work done." At least
that's what I think she says.

The patience of the spider's web
is not disturbed by dew.

Time makes us supplicant whores.
Ray Carver told me he was missing years.
The bottle's iron mouth suckles the brain dry.

Early May mud on my boot soles,
just that much less I have to hoe.

The old Finn (85) walks
twenty-five miles to see his brother.
Why? "I don't have no car."

Look again: that's not
a yellow oak leaf on the path,
but the breastplate from a turtle.

The robins are back,
so weary from flying that they walk
wherever they go.

When we were young we talked
about bottomless lakes, which meant to us
the same lakes were bottomless in China.

You had to milk the cows at 5 a.m.
and 5 p.m. or they'd start bawling.
Even udders can become brutal clocks.

That winter the night fell seven
times a day and horses learned
to run under the ground.

Time flew in and out of the window
until she dropped dead in the kitchen.

At the end, just a pinch of the world
is all we have left to hold on to,
the hem of a sheet.

What if everyone you've loved
were still alive? That's the province
of the young, who don't know it.

A new spring and it's still 5:30
on the cabin's clock. It's always dawn
or time for dinner. My favorites.

If a camel can stretch its muzzle
out of its own stink
so can I.

Lazed on the floor like an old baby
for three hours, then rowed my blue
and brown boat.

Oh, to be in love,
with all five buckets
of the senses
overflowing!

On the shoulder, the turtle
warily holds out his head
on the end of a stick.

The moon, all lordly white,
an anti-rose embedded
at dawn in a thin veil
of red clouds.

Their balls were so swollen they collided
their motorcycles at 70 mph
with only momentary regret.

It's nice to think that when
we're fossils we'll all be in the same
thin layer of rock.

To get to the past,
let's follow the odor of fish
and fried potatoes.

The imagination's kisses
are a cloud of butterflies.

We should
sit like a cat
and wait for the door
to open.

In our farthest field,
between one walk
and the next,
the arrival of ten billion
grasshoppers.

How sharp must be the fletcher's knife
to split a feather
and leave in both halves flight.

The old hen scratches
then looks, scratches then looks.
My life.

Every time I've had a sea change
I thought I was dying.
I probably was.

My stopped clock is always
jumping ahead,
a sure winner in the race with time,
with every day as long as I wish it to be.

A vermilion flycatcher flew too far north
and died in Montana. The same for a Michigan wolf
in Missouri. I get butchered in New York
but don't mind it. I rise again the third day.

Bucket in the rain,
rejoice!

Deerflies die by the billions, the cool air
so clear you drink it in gulps
and the moon drifts closer to the cabin door.

Sometimes fate will steal a baby
and leave an old man
soft as a bundle of rags.

So happy with my fat old body,
still quick enough to slap a fly.

Black dog on white snow
beside the flooding, brown river.
This is where I live!

I feel
the bear's heart
in her footprints.

To have reverence for life
you must have reverence for death.
The dogs we love are not taken from us
but leave when summoned by the gods.

You asked, *What makes you sure?*
I have the faith of the blind,
I answered.

Wish-wash. Ten thousand tons of peanuts
free to us monkeys for 10,000 years.
Oh taste and see, but not in a hurry.

One barred owl harried by
eight loud crows.
A thief besieged by thieves.

A light snow shows
that even the old wagon track
is new.

I hope there's time
for this and that,
and not just this.

Pout and drift. The poet self-sunk
for three months looks up at the dark
heavens, puzzled by moon and stars.

The butterfly's brain,
the size of a grain of salt,
guides her to Mexico.

Buddhists say everything is led by mind.
My doubts are healed by drinking
a bottle of red wine in thirty-three minutes.

DNA shows that I'm the Unknown Soldier.
I can't hear the birds down here,
only politicians shitting out of their mouths.

The water spider
bounces on his legs
but cannot shake the lake.

The low ceiling grazes
the tops of the tall pines
encircling the yard.
Even the air feels crushed.

Peach sky
at sunset,
then (for God's sake)
one leaf across
the big October moon.

Dust too
is drawn on wings
to light.

Last year the snake
left her skin on the floor,
diaphanous like the name
of a lovely girl you've forgotten—
but not her flesh.

I'm sixty-two and can drop dead
at any moment. Thinking this in August
I kissed the river's cold moving lips.

The colder the raindrops
the harder they knock
on the door.

Come to think of it,
there's no reason to decide
who you are.

Stars from horizon to horizon.
A whole half universe
just to light the path.

Rilke says the new year brings things that have
never been, forgetting "won't be again."
Even a dog is never lost in the same place.

Awake in Paris all night listening to rain.
It's lucky there's nothing to eat, a fat dog
waiting for the luck of a roadkill possum.

I prefer the skyline
of a shelf of books.

Imagine a gallery
where all the paintings
opened and closed their wings!

In Brazil I leapt
out of my skin, then back
into it, a onetime-only trick.

Sometimes all it takes
to be happy
is a dime on the sidewalk.

When women pleasure themselves, I heard
at age twelve, they tweak their left ear
then move on to greatness.

Turn over any leaf,
eternity stays always
on the other side.

The moon put her hand
over my mouth and told me
to shut up and watch.

I surely understand paper and how poets
disappear despite it. These days I write
so lightly I don't quite touch it.

A man pays court with his poems.
A woman dismisses him with hers.

Monkeys search each other
and so do we. Another sign
of our advancement.

All those spin butchers drooling
public pus. Save your first
bullet for television.

Rate the hours. One and 5 a.m.
are fine while 3 is the harshest.
The fool always feels safe at noon.

I thought my friend was drinking
too much, but it was the vodka
that was drinking him.

An uncommon number of us die
on our birthdays. You turn a bend
and abruptly you're back home.

Now that I'm older I perfectly
recall the elephant's eye
and the whale's eye that blinked.

That little red eye behind the toilet?
And we think poets
have a baleful look.

This is the county fair
and everything has a bull's ring
through its nose.
Who is leading?

After fifty years of tracking clouds
I've become cold rain upon my life.
How odd to see the mist so clearly.

Autumn dusk, and in the grass
the spiders' gray funnels
drain off the light.

In the electric chair's harness,
one man hauls all the darkness.

Our lives as highlights on TV:
our best lays and meals,
our backward flights of drunken
fancy down the stairs.

These house-trailer fires kill thousands
who will no longer suffer
the opinions and scorn of the rich.

Coming home from the tavern—
I see the pile of dirty clothes
on the cabin floor move.
Doglike, the snake is getting comfortable.

The path disappeared. There was a field
with no edges over which I walked
through the sky which blanketed the ground.

In this lowbrow wilderness
in the area of the black-phase wolf,
I give up my opinions.

A house will turn itself
to catch a little moonlight
on a bedpost.

It's the Devil's
blessing
that flies sleep
at night.

In the house the lizards' enemy
is porcelain. They struggle in the sink.
Warren, the cat, finds them there.

The tree also died the exact
moment the old raven fell off
a lower branch.

A frosty morning,
and one mosquito
at rest on the lip
of the tub.

Sometimes the teakettle rattles
over the flame with the *And! And! And!*
of a child telling a story too big
to pour out all at once.

So the Greeks had amphorae
with friezes of nymphs.
We have coffee mugs with ads
for farm equipment!

How evil all priesthoods.
All over the earth Holy Places
soaked with extra blood.

The handle of its neck
clucks back and forth
and ratchets the turkey
forward.

How is it the rich always know
what is best for the poor?

Trelawny burned Shelley's heart
while thousands of poets
were waiting for transplants.

Lush petals
and glistening thorns—
this college
full of experts.

The poet holds the podium
in both hands
like a garbage bag of words.

See how the rich and famous
sniff the tips of their fingers.
What have they been touching?

Ikkyū was awakened by a crow's caw,
which is not the same as an alarm clock.
He adored the whore dressed in gold brocade.
O master, why count flowers that are gone?

On the nightstand,
a copy of *Prevention* magazine
and the night coming on.

Like an old dog
I slowly lower and arrange myself
in a heap of sighs.

Scientists say the moon grows 1½ inches
farther away every year. I'll fight
this cosmic terrorism hand to hand.

What I learned: Dogs walk upstairs
for nothing. Don't eat with your nose.
Tonight the moon owns this river.

Often I travel at night and am surprised
where I end up at dawn. All road signs and maps
are hoaxes. Don't forget the earth is round.

Earth touched Moon
with his shadow, and Moon
blushed. Everyone saw it.

"When the roll is called up yonder
I'll be there," they sang. Hopefully.
Maybe. But maybe not.

Foolish me,
to think my wine
would never turn.

Come close to death
and you begin to see
what's under your nose.

On the cabin floor a trapped mouse
covers maggots that writhe.
With this in sight,
allow me to squeak.

I've been married since birth.
All other women sense the bottomless
depth of my insincerity.

A breezy March,
so much to learn from laundry
drying on a line.

Without her scarves
the weeping willow
has a twisted body.

They're putting a new green tin roof
on my moss-covered cabin.
Bang, what violence.

It rained so hard the sky became water
and under a mantle of trees I gulped for air.
Here on the bottom the water rose to my chin,
and my face ached to grow gills.

A welcome mat of moonlight
on the floor. Wipe your feet
before getting into bed.

Bullfrog groans.
He is the wooden floor
under the cold feet of the night.

The full moon often rises
in the wrong place. Tonight I sense
activity up there, a general unrest.

My wife's lovely dog, Mary, kills
butterflies. They're easier than birds.
I wonder if Buddha had dog nature.

Three teeth pulled including
a prime buck. Tongue probes
the jaw's lonesome holes.

Alone in the car
we try to tell ourselves
some good news.

These headlights
swim right through
the seine of falling snow.

In our October windfall time, red
apples on frostbitten green grass.
You learn to eat around the wormholes.

As long as the woodpecker
taps on my roof I'll be fine,
a little life left in the shell.

The blind man navigates
by stars behind the daylight.

Just before I fly out of myself
I'll say a puzzled goodbye.
Our bodies are women who were never
meant to be faithful to us.

I was born a baby.
What has been
added?

Treasure what you find
already in your pocket, friend.

Wherever you look in the empty corral
you see the dead pony.

Today a pink rose in a vase
on the table.
Tomorrow, petals.

The pastures grow up
with red cedars
once the horses are gone.

We Were an Unlikely Pair

I met Jim Harrison in the late eighties when he was in Nebraska doing research for his novel *Dalva*. We were introduced by John Carter, then the curator of the photography collection at the state historical society. John was showing Jim boxes of pictures of Nebraska's Old West period, which lasted, with chaps, pistols, and whiskey, until the Great War.

We were an unlikely pair to become friends. I was the sober, thin, anxious businessman-poet, the Stan Laurel of the two of us, and Jim was "The Jim" from the top down, not sober, not thin, not anxious at all—a gruff, blustering, loveable Oliver Hardy.

We three had gluttonous dinners together, at places where Jim could smoke at the table, then I'd go home, and Jim and Carter (we called him Carter, not John) would go watch the pole dancers at The Night Before. Late, Jim would return to his suite at The Cornhusker Hotel, where on one of those stays he got in trouble for smoking in a nonsmoking room. Not actually *in* the room but in the shower, with the water running to dampen the smoke. The author of all those great books fell back on two words, which he used time and again: "Oh, well . . ."

After he left Nebraska with his research notes, he and I began exchanging handwritten letters, which included short, haiku-like poems. I always loved finding a letter from Jim in our box by the road. His handwriting, big and bold, written with a black Pilot Razor Point, was true to his personality. The letters eventually graduated to faxes, which were faster, and Jim's lifelong friend, and my new friend, Dan Gerber, became part of a three-way fax correspondence that lasted till Jim's death in 2016. *Braided Creek* is dedicated to Dan.

After probably a hundred letters or so, Jim suggested we might make a book of the poems, and it fell to me to select and arrange them. I copied each poem onto a three-by-five index card and laid out two very long trails through the living room into the dining room. My wife and I had to step over and around this shifting and riverine manuscript for a couple of weeks. She was typically tolerant.

A number of poems were redundant, and others were clunkers, so I removed those, and shuffled the remaining poems until I had an order that felt like a conversation. I wanted the book to have an underlying momentum, the poems building on each other—connecting, echoing, calling back and forth. I steadfastly avoided alternating the poems—one by Jim, one by me—because that would be metronomic and we'd agreed that we wanted the poems to be anonymous. When I finished my arrangement, I put a manuscript together, sent it to Jim for his comments, and he sent it on to Copper Canyon. The manuscript was warmly received by the press and published in paperback in 2003. It was the first book I published with Copper Canyon, and *Braided Creek* has since gone through multiple printings. Jim and I did several joint readings, and we read back and forth, so that I might read one of Jim's poems and he might read one of mine. We wanted to preserve our anonymity. There's a photograph taken of us reading for the Lannan Foundation in Santa Fe that shows all the fun we were having.

As to that anonymity, we felt that to have each poem signed by its author would break up the book into little stand-alone pieces, and we wanted a smooth flow from cover to cover. It has been great fun to see people speculating about who wrote which poem. One early reviewer wrote something like this: "For those of us familiar with the poems of Jim Harrison and Ted Kooser, it is easy to tell which poet wrote which." Then he went on to cite one of the poems, saying "This one, for example, is clearly by Harrison," and the poem he was citing was by me. Jim and I promised each other that we'd keep the authorship secret, and we have. Truth be told, in some instances I have lost track of who wrote which poem, and I find this curious fact quite pleasant.

My dear friend and correspondent would have delighted in seeing a handsome new edition like this. Inspired by the occasion, I've sent Jim a few new poems that are interspersed throughout. Wouldn't it be wonderful if we get a reply?

Ted Kooser

Garland, Nebraska

About the Poets

Ted Kooser (left) and Jim Harrison, reading from *Braided Creek*.
Photograph courtesy of Don J. Usner.

Ted Kooser once said, "Keeping a journal is like taking good care of one's heart."

Jim Harrison (1937–2016) once said, "Death steals everything except our stories."

The Heart's Work:
Jim Harrison's Poetic Legacy

Copper Canyon Press extends profound gratitude to the following donors and supporters for their foundational investments in the multi-book project The Heart's Work: Jim Harrison's Poetic Legacy. The "Expanded Anniversary Edition" of *Braided Creek: A Conversation in Poetry* is a joyous testament to their commitment and vision.

Joyce Harrington Bahle

Will Blythe

Denver Butson

David Caligiuri

Michael Cashin

Lea Chatham

Russell Chatham

Dr. Mary Lee Coffey

Susann Craig

Michael Croy

Todd Davis

Guy de la Valdene

Michael Delp

Chris Dombrowski

Mary and John ("Nick") Dumsch

Austin Evans

John Evans

Saramel Evans

John Freeman

Dan and Debbie Gerber

David and Cynthia Harrison

James T. Harrison Trust

William R. Hearst III

Anna Harrison Hjortsberg

Judy Hottensen

Lisa and Richard C. Howorth

Amy Hundley and Kristabelle Munson

Dana Jennings

David Johnson

Bruce S. Kahn

Garrison Keillor

George Knotek

Ted Kooser

Peter Lewis and Johnna Turiano

Larry Mawby and Lois Bahle

Colum McCann

Terry McDonell and Stacey Hadash

Liesel and Hank Meijer

Rebecca Newth Harrison

Jack Nicholson

Raúl Niño

Gregg Orr

Molly Phinny

Peter Phinny

Jamie Harrison Potenberg and Steve Potenberg

Red Pine

Amy Reynolds and Victor Herman

Nancy Richard

Randy Riley, Library of Michigan

Joseph Roberts

Paul and Jennifer Saffo

Bud Schulz

J. Stephen Sheppard

Liesl Slabaugh and Joseph Bednarik

Stephen Spencer

Joy Williams

Terry Tempest Williams

Joan Woods

Ray Zepeda

Copper Canyon Press is deeply grateful to the following donors who have directly supported the publication of the "Expanded Anniversary Edition" of *Braided Creek: A Conversation in Poetry*. Each and all have helped make this *Braided Creek* poem a reality for readers they will never meet:

A book on the arm of my chair
and the morning before me.

Porter Abbott

Ginny Agnew

Blaine Allan

Virginia Anderson

In memory of Thomas Shan Arnold

Joyce Harrington Bahle

Peter David Birt

Will Blythe

Boar and Badger Society of TN

Peter Bodlaender

Brant Brechbiel

David Brewster and Mary Kay Sneeringer in honor of Mary Jane Brewster

Therese Broderick

Diana Broze

Deborah Buchanan

Dan and Lorraine Burns

Frank Buxton

Jean E. MacLaren Calandra

Chapters Books & Gifts

Harriett Cody and Harvey Sadis

Sheri Sherman Cohen

Elizabeth J. Coleman

Coley, Kati, and Mike Conklin

Keith R. Courtad

Keith Cowan and Linda Walsh

Bradley Scott Davis

Susan DeWitt Davie

Karen Dhyanchand

Alexander Diederich

Andrew and Elizabeth Dreszer

Martin Dudley

Mary and John ("Nick") Dumsch

Rhae Eaton

John Albert Ehrenfried

Ann Ehringhaus

Art Elser

John Evans

Nancy M. Faaren

Dan Fahrbach

In memory of John Carter and Katherine Farrell

Michael Ferreboeuf

Ross Field

Foster-Petroska

Julie Fowler

Mira Yli Fox

Bob Francis

John Freeman

Mary Beth Frezon

Mimi Gates

Leirion Gaylor Baird

Danny Gillane

In memory of Annie Gordon

Rita Gram

Anne Griffin

Alexandra Guequierre Klodenski

Art Hanlon

John Harmon

David and Cynthia Harrison

Linda Healy

Eileen Heidenheimer

Stephen D. Hill

David Himber

Thomas A. Hinds

Steven Hopkins

Judy Hottensen

Rob and Sally Jackson

Duane Jensen

David Jacob Kader

Bruce S. Kahn

Richard Katz

Clint King

In memory of Jim Kirk

KJM

George Knotek

Veronica Kornberg

Brett and Cristy Krablin

Marty Krasney

Anne Kundtz
Patti Kwok
Chris La Tray
Tom Lakin
Lemuria Bookstore
Peter Lewis and Johnna Turiano
John and Margy Ligon
Andrew Littauer
Bill and Kathy Lydiatt
Catherine Marchiando
Erik Ira Phillip Jordan Mayberg
Jonathan Noah Mayberg
Nathan Mayer Mayberg
Molly McNulty
Rodger Moody
Chatham Morgan
Elizabeth Mornin
Joseph P. Morra
Karla K. Morton
William Andrew Muller
Joan L. Murphy
Mark Musto
Nick Neely
Jennifer and Jamie Newton
Vergil E. Noble
Dennis Noson
In memory of Madison Cloudfeather Nye

Sharon L. Oriel
H.C. Palmer
Walter Parsons
James Payne
Nancy and Charles Peek
Brian Perry
Marc Petrie
Frank Pommersheim
Jamie Harrison Potenberg and Steve Potenberg
Laura Price Kennedy
Adrian and Molly Rice
Patricia Richardson
Lawrence Ridley
Mary P. Riordan
Jeanmarie Riquelme
Sara and Tripp Ritter
Vernon and Sharon Ritzman
Joseph Roberts
Thomas Robison
John Rosenberg
Jeffery David Ross
StanleydelGozo Sabre
Kenneth Sallows
Pamela J. Sampel
Heather Saunders Estes
Timothy Schaffner
Wilfried Schubert and Family
Eric Schulte

Scott Schutte
Kim and Jeff Seely
Jon and Trudy Shumaker
Randall S. Smith
Annie Snider
Gwendolyn and Stan Soper
In memory of Rosalie Sorrels
Scott Owen Sprunger
Gregory L. Stidham, MD
Sarah B. Sullivan
Yolanda Danyi Szuch
Eddie Tadlock
Ron and Gail Trendler
Brett Van Emst
Maria Van Newkirk
Kelly Vande Plasse
Elizabeth Anne Verink
Donna Vincenti
Miriam Weinstein
Doug Wick and Lucy Fisher
Jennifer Wilson
Debra Winger
Warren Woessner
Paul Woodruff
Wesley Yard
Ray Zepeda

Poetry is vital to language and living. Since 1972, Copper Canyon Press has published extraordinary poetry from around the world to engage the imaginations and intellects of readers, writers, booksellers, librarians, teachers, students, and donors.

WE ARE GRATEFUL FOR THE MAJOR SUPPORT PROVIDED BY:

  Lannan

Richard Andrews and Colleen Chartier
Anonymous (2)
Jill Baker and Jeffrey Bishop
Anne and Geoffrey Barker
Donna Bellew
Matthew Bellew
Will Blythe
John Branch
Diana Broze
John R. Cahill
Sarah Cavanaugh
Keith Cowan and Linda Walsh
Stephanie Ellis-Smith and
    Douglas Smith
Mimi Gardner Gates
Gull Industries Inc. on behalf of
    William True
William R. Hearst III
Carolyn and Robert Hedin
David and Jane Hibbard
Bruce S. Kahn
Phil Kovacevich and Eric Wechsler
Lakeside Industries Inc. on behalf of
    Jeanne Marie Lee
Maureen Lee and Mark Busto

Peter Lewis and Johnna Turiano
Ellie Mathews and Carl Youngmann as
    The North Press
Larry Mawby and Lois Bahle
Hank and Liesel Meijer
Jack Nicholson
Petunia Charitable Fund and
    adviser Elizabeth Hebert
Madelyn S. Pitts
Suzanne Rapp and Mark Hamilton
Adam and Lynn Rauch
Emily and Dan Raymond
Joseph C. Roberts
Jill and Bill Ruckelshaus
Cynthia Sears
Kim and Jeff Seely
Nora Hutton Shepard
Arthur Sze
D.D. Wigley
Joan F. Woods
Barbara and Charles Wright
In honor of C.D. Wright,
    from Forrest Gander
Caleb Young as C. Young Creative
The dedicated interns and faithful
    volunteers of Copper Canyon Press

TO LEARN MORE ABOUT UNDERWRITING COPPER CANYON PRESS TITLES,
PLEASE CALL 360-385-4925 EXT. 103

The pressmark for Copper Canyon Press
suggests entrance, connection, and interaction
while holding at its center
an attentive, dynamic space for poetry.

This book is set in Adobe Jenson Pro Light.
Book design by Gopa & Ted2, Inc.
Printed on archival-quality paper.

Braided Creek was first published in paperback in 2003.
The original version also appeared in a signed, limited edition of
250 numbered copies. An additional 26 copies were
lettered A to Z with holograph poems by each poet.